Tales from Low Newton Jail

Edited by
Helen Aitchison

Write on the Tyne

First published in Great Britain in 2025 by Write on the Tyne CIC.

Printed and bound by Amazon

Paperback ISBN: 978-1-0682274-0-0

Cover image: designed by a prisoner at HMP Low Newton

Published by Write on the Tyne
www.writeonthetyne.com

Foreword

HMP/YOI Low Newton is a prison located in Durham, North-East England, for female adult and young offenders who have faced multiple disadvantages including substance misuse, homelessness, mental health challenges, domestic abuse, and interactions with the criminal justice system. The collaborative vision of Novus Education and HMPPS, is to create a culture of empowerment, social enterprise, and employability that nurtures self-confidence and supports everyone to realise their potential.

In August 2024, Novus Education, HMPPS Low Newton and guest author, Helen Aitchison began a visionary collaboration, aimed at enriching learning opportunities across the prison — through workshops designed to explore gratitude, empowerment, and using writing for well-being and recovery.

This collection of written pieces is a way to share real stories, reflections, and recovery of those with lived experiences, to increase self-esteem, celebrate success, and challenge preconceptions. The creativity, honesty, strength, and positivity is truly empowering.

Kathryn Burton, Local Education Manager, Novus, HMP/YOI Low Newton

Jamie Marsden, Quality Manager, Novus

Please note : pieces have been anonymised to protect the identity of prisoners and their families.

Contents

Behind the Door

We are sitting in our pads, day by day,
thinking of the words we can't say.
Key chains rustling, prisoners screaming,
I know this is real but it feels like I'm dreaming.
Days feel long but the weeks go fast,
hope to get out soon as I don't think I'll last.
Keep your chin up and your chest out,
if you don't, they'll mess you about.
In and out our rooms throughout the day,
but not like kids going outside to play.
Keep your head down, you can do that,
don't cause bother and act like a prat.
Or you'll spend longer behind the door,
and you don't want that any more.

Being Strong

In the past, I have had a big problem with drugs. However, in prison, I have worked with the drug team and they've helped me. I'm no longer on drugs or the methadone programme. I will keep working with the drug team in Low Newton and continue working with support services in the community, when I'm released.

There are many times in my life that I have had to be strong. My children were taken from my care and I had to be strong during that heartbreaking time. I was on my own but I kept going. Now, I know I am strong and I will continue to cope. I will always hold my head up high and take what life throws at me, knowing I am strong.

Chains

I loved you all once.
I lost you all,
to drugs and bitter pain.
But don't fret,
one day, one by one,
our chains will link again.

Crack

Channelling my feelings to improve my life.
Reconnecting with my support network.
Achieving my goals that mean the most to me.
Caring about others who need help in their journey.
Keep climbing. There is no drug that gives you the feeling of achieving in life!

Dear… (Letters)

Dear A,

Thank you. Because of you, I'm so much stronger. I know now how I should have been treated and not settled for less. I'm grateful that you are in the past, and that is where you are staying.

I now have amazing boyfriend, who treats me right. I feel sorry for you. You tried to destroy me, just so you could feel better about yourself. But you lost and I won. I found so much strength in me that I didn't know I had.

The best thing that came from us is our kids.

Dear A,

Hi, babe. How are you doing? Good, I hope. I'm going to see my barrister today, so I hope it's good news. We could do with some.

How are you and your pad mate getting on? What's he called? Do I know him? I hope you know how much I love you and miss you every day. I can't wait to see you and I can't wait until we are home and get a house sorted out. A nice, fresh start.

Love you loads.

Speak soon.

xxx

Dear Dad and Mam,

Dad, I miss you,

And you will never be forgotten.

Dad, I love you.

xxx

Mam, I love you,

And respect you,

More and more each day.

xxx

Dear E,

I'm so sorry I let you down. I'm sorry that I wasn't there at the end. I love you more than life and I miss you with every breath that I take. Not a day goes by where I don't think about you and what you would be doing now.

It's hard to believe that you would be twenty-one, as it feels like forever since you died. F misses you so much, as do all of your friends. You would have been so proud of them all at your funeral, as they carried your coffin.

I wish I could swap places with you. You didn't deserve to die; you were just a baby. Tell Mum and Dad that I miss them.

I love you.

Your big sister.

xxx

Dear Dad,

I love you to bits. You are the funniest person I have ever met. You've always made me laugh and still do. I have so many good memories of you and times with you, and I love spending time together, chatting and laughing.

I can't wait to see you again, Dad. To make new memories together. I know you are in a care home because of your stroke, but you are strong, Dad. This comes from the heart and I love you to bits.

Your daughter.

xxx

Dear D,

We were together for four and a half years until I came to jail. When I found out we were pregnant, I was so happy. Then social services became involved. They told me that if I wanted to keep the baby, I would have to stop seeing you.

After a twenty-eight-day recall to prison, I was released and returned home. I went back home, where my family are. The time came for my scan and I was informed that I was having a baby boy. As the months passed, I got ready to give birth to my son and eventually, beautiful A was born.

You only got to see your son three times. When A was ten months old, you took your own life on the train tracks. Your son had lost you and so had I. My life fell apart that day and after three years clean from drugs and working on myself, I relapsed.

My son was taken from my care at fourteen months old. Luckily, my sister has him and he is such a happy boy. I see him all the time and he is a beautiful boy, and I'm grateful he is with her. He looks so much like you: his dad. Your family don't see him, I hope they decide they want to in the future.

I wish I could turn back time and you were here. So that you could see your precious boy growing up. I miss you. I love you always. Until we meet again.

xxx

Dear Family,

I would like you all to know that I love so much. You are one of the only good things to have come from me and you are always there for me. Sometimes, I don't deserve it because I know I have put you three through a lot, but you all stay.

I want nothing more than to make you all proud of me. I've let you down in the past, I'm sorry. I'm going to do my best when I get out of here to make you all happy and proud. A fresh start, making new memories together with you all and my grandkids.

I love you all so much and I couldn't be prouder of each of you. I appreciate what you have done for me, it means a lot.

Love always,

Mam.

xxx

Dear Family,

Prison saved me as I was at a point in my life where I was past caring about anything. I was committing crime to pay for my drug addiction every day and my family were terrified I would die soon.

When I started thinking clearly, I realised how bad everything had become and the impact on my family. I now know where I was going wrong. I can put myself in the shoes of my family, and understand how they felt.

I'm sorry and I'm using my time in prison to work on myself, for myself and my family.

xxx

Dear Family,

I am sorry for letting you three beautiful girls down. I was supposed to be the strong one, but instead, you were all strong. I was supposed to be the one you could all count on, but instead, I counted on you all. I was supposed to be your role model, but instead you are all mine.

I will forever be sorry for not being the person you can all look up to, but I will also forever try and make it up to each of you. I promise, one day soon, you will all be able to finally tell me that you are proud of me — and that will be the day I'll be truly proud of myself.

I love you three so much.

Lots of love,

Mum.

xxx

Dear Family,

My four precious, beautiful baby boys. You will never ever understand how much I love you all. You are all my heart and soul. I love you all to infinity and beyond and you make me the proudest mam on this whole planet.

I always thought I knew what love was until I had you all. I don't need money, because I am the richest woman to walk this earth for being your mam.

Love you all,

Mam.

xxx

Dear Family,

You two are both my special lads. I love you two more than any other people in the world. My most precious days, when you were both born — the best things in my life. You've made me the happiest mother ever. I love you so much and always will.

Things became a struggle for me and after so long, the cracks began to show and it started to go wrong. I made many mistakes, which caused problems, hurt, and distress. I wish this never involved and affected you two, but sadly they did.

I can't change what I've done, whether it's good or bad. However, I can have hope for our future and pray every day things will be better — maybe so good that we will be together again, someday real soon.

Love,

Mam.

xxx

Dear Future Me,

I want to tell you that you don't have to be ashamed of who you are or the things that you have done in your past. It wasn't all your fault but it gave you a wake-up call. Now, you are making things right and you are strong. You'll be able to make up for the bad things, achieve your goals, and create a better life.

You can do it, you have a chance. Your life will be what you make of it.

With love.

xxx

Dear Future Me,

You don't ever have to be alone. There are positive, good people around. Please remember, you don't need drugs or people around you that don't really care about you. One day soon, you will wake up and not think about drugs or alcohol. Instead, you will be thinking about whether you should walk to work or take the car.

You will be studying again, back at university, or working towards getting there. Thinking about your dream career. You'll have passed your driving test and have the freedom of a car. You'll be able to afford to take your daughters away on holiday. Somewhere warm, with lots to do. And you'll be able to spoil them.

Life will be calm and rewarding, I promise. You'll have time and the headspace to help people who are struggling and are where you were — needing support and guidance. You'll get there and you'll use your experiences to help other people. You can do it!

With love.

xxx

Dear Future Me,

I want to tell you that the mistakes you've made haven't been made by choice. Time has flown by and life changes. You've often felt like you haven't had a voice and few people to trust during challenging times. But you've got through it, stronger. Hard feelings and times come and go.

You've managed when most of your friends wouldn't have known what was going on, or what to do and say. You lost your strength at times, unable to take anymore and ended up in prison — and it became somewhere that you called home.

But it will be different. You can do it, because you are strong and your life will be better!

With love.

xxx

Dear Future Me,

I want to tell you that your life as a criminal will not always be that way. You will change. You will move your life forward and try and help others in the way that you have never been helped.

You will make a difference to your own life and to other people's lives. Your life will get better and change as you get older. You'll not always be a drug user — you'll make it!

With love.

xxx

Dear Future Me,

I want to tell you that when the day comes to be out of this place, take every option that comes to you. You've struggled and it's time to down roots — just keep that in mind. You will be happier. You will grow. You will be happy with the man you know.

You'll have the life you have dreamt of because you have put in the hard work. You can be calm, stress-free, loved, and happy. You can be everything you've been thinking you can, because you have A, S, and E.

Your life will be the best you've ever known. So, take each step day by day, and be happy with yourself. Because you've done it, you've made it!

With love.

xxx

Dear Future Me,

I want to tell you that you have had a hell of a life! Things have been hard and you've been through a traumatic time. But you're strong, you will get through this, and things will come together. You can overcome any obstacle that comes your way, you've proved that.

You can make a family, different to the awful one you were born into, and you can do anything that you put your mind to. Once you do, this will be your life and it will be stress-free, loving, and with lots of memories being made. Life will be great!

With love.

xxx

Dear G,

Thank you for sending me to jail. It was only ever good thing you've done for me. I am stronger than you will ever know and I know that I will be better in myself because of this experience.

See you never,

your ex-wife.

Dear Grandma,

I remember every Sunday when you used to make Sunday dinner for us all. It would be me, my family, and friends — we would make a 12-a-side footy team and play football before dinner was cooked. We would laugh and joke, then we would all eat together.

You're no longer here, Grandma, and neither is Dad, but it's a lovely memory that I have.

I love you.

xxx

Dear J,

I hope you are good. I just want to let you know I love you and I am really grateful that you are still standing by my side after everything that has been said and done.

I don't tell you enough how much I love you and appreciate you, and everything you do.

Lots of love,

Mum.

xxx

Dear J,

I love you so, so much. You are my rock. You always know what to say and do to make me smile. If I'm having a bad day, you always make me go to a better place in my mind.

I can't imagine my life without you. You and my children are my world. I can't wait to get out of here to make a future for us all.

Love you lots.

xxx

Dear Kids,

Hi, I hope you are okay. Mum misses you loads and I can't wait to come home and see you all. It's hard in here, I cry and I struggle to cope, but I am looking forward to being back home to my babies. It will be so lovely to see you and hear about what you have been doing. Hopefully, you're keeping well. Not long until I see you, my babies.

Love,

your mum.

xxx

Dear Mam,

If I could go back in time, I'd take your advice and not hold anything against you. All the times you tried to guide and support me, and just love me. You tried to teach me right from wrong. I thought I knew best. Well, I didn't know best. I believe your wise words of, 'Mother always knows best.'

You have been the only constant role model in my life and showed me how to be a better, kinder person when the world is not so nice. The woman I am today, is the woman and daughter you wanted me to be. Thank you for sticking by me and making me a strong woman.

You were always there, wiping my tears as a child. When I would fall, you'd cover my grazes with plasters and love. And you cared for me as an adult, helping heal my heart ache. It is true what they say: a mother's and daughter's love and bond is the most precious gift. I am lucky to have a mother like you. If mams were flowers, I'd pick you every time. Now I'm older, I realise and understand all you ever wanted was the best for me and to make you proud.

It's my time to look after you. You deserve the world, Mam. Thank you for everything you did for us. Even through the hard times, you got on with it. We always saw a brave, happy mam who wanted her children to be happy. If I could be the woman you are, I would be proud. I'm lucky to have you as my mam.

Lots of love, your daughter.

xxx

Dear Mam,

I love you and miss you every day. Your passing has left me lost and lonely. You had a rough life but you never gave up. I want to let you know that I am going to make you proud — just like you made me proud to be your daughter.

You were the best mam ever and I will be back in your arms when we meet again. You are an inspiration to me because you never gave up on us. Even when we were in care, you would travel to see us. You always fed us before you fed yourself and if there wasn't enough, we would share. You did us proud.

I love you so much, forever and always. Until we meet again, my angel.

xxx

Dear Mam,

I know I don't tell you enough how much I respect you, and that I am grateful for all that you do for me and my two girls. I don't tell you enough how much you mean to me and all I want to do for you is to make you proud of me. You're an amazing mam and I love you millions.

All my love.

xxx

Dear Mam,

I want to thank you for never turning your back on me. It doesn't matter what I have done, or any drug that I turned to in order to try and deal with the pain of my ex keeping my children, you never hated me. You always loved me.

I want to thank you for always being there for me but also for always being there for my family. I want you to know that you are the reason I am still here today, because of your love and support.

Thank you so much, Mam, I will never forget what you have done for me. I love you with all of my heart, forever and always.

Love, your daughter.

xxx

Dear Mam,

I am writing this letter to tell you how much I am thankful for your support. If it wasn't for you, Mam, I really don't know where I would be in life. Thank you so much for all your love and help.

Now it's my time to help you and look after you — because I would walk the length of the world for you. Mam, you are the only one that I have left in my life, so it is time to live our lives to the max! It's time to be happy and start to do things together.

I love you, Mam.

xxx

Dear Mam,

I'm so grateful for you. I don't know how I would have gotten through this without you. Thank you for standing by me. Even when I tried to push everyone away.

We have had our ups and downs, but our bond is strong. Thank you for financially supporting me, even though I know you struggle. I love you so much and I'm so grateful.

Love, your daughter.

xxx

Dear Mam,

Thanks, Mam, for sticking by me. I knew you would, to be honest, because of who you are. You have always been my best friend and you have never turned your back on me once, even though I've done some stupid things in my life.

Thank you, Mam.

I love you.

xxx

Dear Mam,

Finally, I've found myself, and it feels so good to be in control. I feel free and I know that I'm not alone, as you have been on this journey with me — every step of the way.

Thank you, Mam.

I love you.

xxx

Dear Mama Bear,

Hopefully, when this is published, I can show you myself. But if not, I'm still going to read it to you. I want to thank you for everything that you've done for me, and helped me with. For always listening to me, and just letting me into your life and heart. You will always be in my heart and soul. I'm going to be there for you, until the end — and I'm honoured that I'm one of the very few you trust to be by your side.

You have shown me strength in ways that I didn't know. I thought that I knew every kind of strength down to a T, but the strength I see every day in you, is admirable. You're the only person that I've ever looked at as a mother figure. I lost my mam at fourteen and although no one can replace her, having you as a mam too, has been amazing.

For the rest of my life, you're my inspiration. My kids will learn who you are and what you mean to me. They'll learn the strength from me that you've given me. Your advice will guide me through life and I will always know that you are with me. My you-shaped hole in my heart will be my subconscious, keeping me right in life, you: my guardian angel. I love you so much and I always will. I know I'll crumble first but I know that is not what you want.

So, I promise that when I feel like I am crumbling, I will think of the laughs that we have had every single day. I'll cherish all the memories with you — good and bad, because that's what makes us family forever and always.

I love you, my angel.

xxx

Dear M,

Here are a few things I need you to know. I know you have been through a lot, losing your mam and C when you were just a kid, and not having many people to confide in a lot of the time, during other things that you've gone through. Then losing your hero, your rock — and you thinking that you have no one.

I just want you to know that you are loved. You are not alone and I am here for you no matter what. I can't wait to move on past this chapter in our lives. So, hold your head high because you are stronger than you think.

And you make me want to do better in life and to make better memories. You make me a better person and to know what I want in life; to have and grow our own family.

Love always.

xxx

Dear My Handsome Man,

Hello there, love of my life!
It's just me, your future wife.
I love you now and always will.
I'll nurse you through times you're ill.
You bring me love.
You bring me joy.
You are my handsome, sexy boy!

xxx

Dear M,

Thank you for being there for me, despite being through so much yourself from such a young age. You lost your first baby, then your sight, and you lost your mum and dad. You've had it really hard, yet you have still supported other people and cared for them.

You've always been an amazing mum and grandmother to my daughter. You've been a mother-figure to me, even at times when I definitely did not deserve the support. You are such a special person and you've always shown me loyalty, care, and love. Thank you.

Lots of love.

xxx

Dear Nana,

I wish you were still here. I know you are always with me, like a guardian angel. And I know you try to warn me when things are bad. I wish I would have listened to you in the past.

I miss you loads but thank you for teaching me so much. You taught me how to bake and so much more. I can't believe you left so young. Thank you, Nana, for being you. I love and miss you.

xxx

Dear Nana and Grandad,

Thank you for bringing me up and looking after me. I had everything I needed, everything I wanted, and more. I felt so loved. You were both always there whenever I needed to shout and scream, or if I needed to talk. You both made sure that I did something with my life and tried new things.

However, when I lost you both, I went down the wrong track. I really regret this and I'm sorry. Sitting here now, I can see that I messed up. I will turn things around Nana and Grandad, for you both, and to thank you for everything you did for me. I will have a better future.

Love always.

xxx

Dear N,

You are my world. I never thought we would be in this position but I am eternally grateful to you for holding it all together with your mam, brother, and partner in prison. You've looked after us all as well as been there for your own four-year-old daughter going through surgery. Alongside having a job and house to manage.

I could not be any prouder of you. I always ask how you cope and you say it's because I am your mam and I taught you what to do. But in truth, I will never be as strong as you. Keep being you! I love you.

Love,

Mam.

xxx

Dear P,

I miss you. I remember the first time we met. I walked into the pub and asked if you wanted to play pool. Then in the next pub, you walked in when I was sitting with my friends.

We got talking and had a good laugh. You told me all about your life and that you worked in the local college. We got on so well and we moved in together.

I miss you so much.

With love.

xxx

Dear Son,

When I get out of here, I promise, I will change my life. We are both still healthy and safe — to me, that means everything. To the world you are one person, but to me, you are the world.

Love you forever,

Mam.

xxx

Dear Unknown,

If I wrote this, it must be that you're on my mind, right?
You've got me sat here thinking about old times.
And all the times you made me laugh,
oh, how I smiled till it hurt.
There's so much love inside of these words.
Say no more, you know,
don't talk too much.
Short and sweet.

With love.

xxx

Dear Younger Me,

Everything will eventually get better. Nothing is bigger than God — hand it over to him. Guard your heart and don't judge yourself too harshly. Start to love yourself; it's easier said than done, believe me, I know! But before anyone can love you, you need to love yourself.

Stop worrying too much about what other people think. They will come and go in your life and you can't please everyone all of the time. So stop trying. Treat your family better, especially your dad. He's your best friend and he deserves better for being in your future life. If you can find a man like him, do everything you can to keep him.

Listen to people's advice. Don't think you always know better and that they don't know what it's like. They are trying to help you, not to preach. Stay true to yourself and keep strong.

Lots of love,

Me.

xxx

Dear Younger Me,

I have some things to say. Make sure you listen to the advice you are given, because you'll need it when you are older. Adults have the experience and it's not that they are trying to tell you what to do, it's because often, they have been there and they want to set you on the right path. They know more about life than you think you do.

It's not them having a go at you, complaining. It is life advice. So, listen now, before you wished in the future that you had.

Love from,

Me.

xxx

Drugs

Dream of my life ahead,
Recovering from my demons.
Understanding how I feel, drug free.
Going on and feeling freedom.
Strength is how I feel being drug free.

Existing

Why was I born? Why do I even exist?
It's been a life of hell and misery.
All the pain I have suffered, all the pain I have caused,
and you wonder why my heart is torn.
All the lows and very few highs,
all those memories that flow.
It's like a tap that won't turn off,
I wish it would stop.
Always wanting to end my life, as it's the easy way out.
But then I stop and think of my kids.
I can't keep living this life of hell,
I've always felt different to everyone else.
No one cares, I don't belong.
Will my life ever get better?
Can I ever change?
Is this all life has to offer me?
I think it's time for professional help.

Family

For all the money in the land,
All I want to do,
Maybe get a car,
I would drive straight to you.
Listen to what I'm saying,
You know, I'm always praying.

Feathers from an Angel

Angels look over us,
protect us from ourselves.
Feathers are left for us to find.
So, if you find a feather, make a wish.
As your angel will hear it,
and change it into dreams.

Feelings

I know I am moody and hard work.
I chip myself away, like her wood bark work.
My feelings are real and truly strong,
so I ask of her, please hold on.
Times are hard, but will be fine,
because in the end, we will shine.
It's time to leave our past behind,
because me and my girl, are one of a kind.
Look forward to our future and don't hold back,
because if we don't there's no coming back.
All of the little divs, there's no going back.

Friends

The friends I've made,
the girls I know.
They pick me up,
when I'm feeling low.
They know before I even cry,
they pick me up and make me smile.
So, for my girls,
I'd like to say.
Thanks for being there,
day-to-day.

Getting Support

I was born in Newcastle and remained living there until I came to prison. There is a lot of help in Newcastle, but still not enough for all the people needing support. Services like Changing Lives, Crisis, and Plummer Court, provide support around homelessness and addiction, many with staff who have experienced similar issues.

I've experienced addiction and homelessness. I've lived in hostels in Newcastle and they have provided support to me and many other women. Once I leave prison, I will need that support once more, as I will be homeless. It's difficult going through the process again, and the worry of ending up on the streets is real. Having nowhere to live is the biggest challenge. You can't begin to work through other issues without somewhere safe to stay.

Having accommodation means people can work with services around their addiction or mental health. I have previously worked with addiction services and also accessed Crisis, who help people around homelessness but also provide addiction support. I was able to attend classes there and they offer cooking and art classes, film nights, and support sessions where people can talk through problems. It was nice to be around people who understood what I was going through.

When I leave prison, I hope I can get somewhere safe to stay to be able to work with services in my area. I want to move on and reach my goals.

Grieving

I've suffered with bereavement issues for many years. Losing my beloved mam to cancer. Watching her deteriorate and fade away within six short months, was heartbreaking. She told me that she wasn't afraid of dying but she was scared to leave her four children. All she wanted was to have her four kids around her one last time before she left us.

Me and my older sister, were there all the time. However, my brother, and other sister, were both in prison at the time. They were allowed to come home and visit us and see Mam. But they were only allowed one at a time, so it was really hard with my mam repeatedly asking for us all to be together so she could see us all one last time. It was heartbreaking to let her down and I was sad that the system could not accommodate this important ask.

Mam hung on as long as she possibly could. Watching her fade away each day was so bad. I can't imagine how hard it was for my sister and brother, who were not there with Mam, like we were. They must have struggled with losing our mam whilst they were in prison.

At the time, when Mam was dying, I had been clean for four years. As a way of coping, I relapsed and started using drugs again. They blocked it all out and then the drugs took over and crime crept in. It soon got so bad that I couldn't give it up and not long after we lost our mam, I ended up back in prison. After so many times of coming here, it has started to feel that it's the place where I belong.

Growing

I've come a long way. I came to prison frightened, vulnerable, and an emotional wreck. Straight to E Wing — *why was I surrounded by these people? I'm different.* Or so I thought. Scared, petrified to come out of my cell the next day. But the girls told me I would be okay, that things will get better.

'Just keep your head down.'

And that's exactly what I did. Six months later, I am a different person. I'm not afraid anymore. That little room that frightened me is now my safe place. I'm doing my time for the biggest mistake of my life. I've acknowledged what I did was wrong. So, while I am here, I must do everything I possibly can to make my life better for my release.

Hartlepool Lass

I'm from Hartlepool and I've experienced a lot in my life that has been difficult. I have experienced domestic abuse and sexual violence, including rape. When I was fourteen years old, I was in a relationship with a twenty-five-year-old. I fell pregnant to him when I was fifteen. Turning sixteen in the March, I had my baby in the April. I gave birth to my beautiful baby — a precious, tiny baby girl.

I loved being a young mam. However, I had some difficulties in my family and my mam was always jealous of me. As I grew up, she would cause problems and when I became a mother, she continued to cause issues. Social services got involved and my baby girl was removed from my care and went to the care of my parents.

This had a massive impact on my mental health and I turned to drugs to try and cope with my loss. Then I met a man who I knew from when I was younger and we got into a relationship. During this time, I ended up using and becoming addicted to heroin and committing a lot of crime to feed my habit. It resulted in me going to prison.

This has become a cycle for me and I am now thirty-six years old and have been to jail thirty times. I hope in the future I can get the right help to change my life and break this pattern.

Homeless

I've been homeless on and off for many years, almost twenty, in fact. And I've been in and out of prison. During my first ever jail sentence, I lost my nana. She was the person that brought me up and I was heartbroken. I really struggled but I got support for my mental health, including counselling, and I got through it.

Being homeless is a big problem. I've had no accommodation when I've left prison. Many times, I have returned back to the streets and then ended up back in prison: a revolving door. I would commit crime to get remanded — this is where I felt safe. I can't handle being on the streets. No one should have to. I'm going to keep fighting for accommodation and to make sure I have a chance when I get out.

Hope

Happiness
Optimism
Purpose
Exciting

Keep Being Strong

I began a course in health and social care at university in 2018. I had ambitions of what I wanted for a career and was studying hard. When I was only a few assignments away from completing the academic year, I met a man.

We got into a relationship and I started drinking heavily. As the relationship progressed, it became abusive and my partner was controlling and violent towards me. I left that relationship but due to my mental health and alcohol misuse, I ended up in a relationship with another man, and we began smoking crack together.

Now I am in here, and I have been working through my addiction issues. I will continue to do this and be strong — with the hope of getting through my life without being under the influence of drugs and alcohol, and be happy and safe.

Keeping Going

When I was thirteen years old, I experienced a problem that became progressively worse. I had a slight soreness in my left eye and as the years passed, I developed cataracts. I ended up losing my sight and to this day, I don't know how. The consultant advised me there was no way to repair my eye and the alternative would be a glass eye.

I had to keep going. I was only young when my vision problems started and as a young adult, when I should have been having fun and learning about life, I was partially sighted, before becoming blind. It led me to many problems, including drugs and alcohol misuse, and crime. But I won't give up. I will keep going and make a future that is positive for myself and my family. I have goals and dreams, and I know I can achieve them.

Life Saver

Waking up here was a good thing. I was alive and breathing, thank God. My parents received a phone call telling them I was in prison and not dead. When the officer phoned my mam to say I was in prison, by the time the officer passed the phone over to me, my mam had passed the phone to my dad. My dad asked if I was okay. In the background, my mam said that she couldn't believe that I was in prison.

The following day, I phoned and I was extremely happy that my mam answered my call. It was such a relief, as I thought that she was totally done with me. It was in that moment that I knew I had to turn my life around for the better. My parents had the best night's sleep and felt more settled than they had in the past eight months — when I had been on the missing persons list. I'd been homeless, as the system failed me. I was on the streets of my home town, the town I was born and raised in, homeless.

Walking around I was wondering what I was going to do, as well as a thousand other things running through my mind. I saw more people homeless; it was a scary place to be. Days and months went by with me being homeless and I ended up drinking alcohol and taking drugs. I had totally lost myself as well as losing my family and friends, barring one of my life-long friends (you know who you are).

Thank you for standing by me, especially the state I was in. I was in a place where I was beyond admitting I needed help. Prison may not be the best place to be, but it has without any doubt, saved my life.

Love is…

Love is happy.
Love is hard.
Love is stress.
Love is pure.
Love is everything.
Love is sad.
Love is different.
Love is unconditional.
Love is love.

Love

Love can be stressful,
it can also be sad.
It can make you feel happy,
it can make you feel glad.
The way love is,
nobody knows.
Everyone's different,
in the way that love shows.

Low Newton (Voices of Prisoners)

A positive about being in Low Newton is that you talk to people who you wouldn't if you were outside. Here, I feel part of a family and have made friends for life. I have routine, discipline, and structure, which helps me, and others. Being in prison has given me time to think. I've been able to make positive family connections and work on myself.

If someone is in prison for the first time, I would advise them to talk to someone, especially the staff — who all help as much as possible.

If someone is in prison for the first time, I would tell them to focus on themselves and not worry about what is going on outside — as this makes it harder to get on with your sentence. Keep talking with girls who will support you and you support them. You can get through it.

Friendships are made in prison. We meet new girls and become better friends than friendships we had at home.

You have structure in prison: stability, a safety net, as well as routine. You end up becoming close to people you least expect to. Sort of like a close family. In prison, yes, it is punishment but it's also punishment when you are ready to leave with nowhere to go. Things should be planned to help stop girls messing up on the outside and then returning, as they have nowhere to call home; no routine, and no support on the outside. It's setting people up to fail and more can and needs be done to help women succeed outside of prison.

Mum

I could write about my mum forever. With her, words aren't enough. My mother is my inspiration and always will be. She is so hardworking and strong. She has always put my needs first and allowed me to travel the world from a young age. And even when I mess up, she's always by my side, supporting me.

She's the best grandmother to my two babies — looking after them whilst I'm in prison, and still running her two businesses. She's a true queen who has the biggest heart. I would give my life to her. She's a diamond that I'll cherish forever. I love you, Mum.

My Future

In the future, I don't want much. All I want is all I have ever wanted — a home to call my own. A nice little flat that I can decorate myself. Some furniture to put my things and know they won't go missing for once. Then, I can actually have things that I can keep, that mean something to me.

I've lost a lot; a lot of my things that I held close. Things that held memories and it's sad. Before I came here, I had nothing left. All I want is to start again and be happy.

My Mam

My mam inspires me. She has stood by me all my life and is the backbone of our family. My mam goes out of her way to help. She's also brought my own children up whilst I've been in prison.

I would say thank you to her, for being the best mam I could wish for. I love you, Mam.

My Message to you

My message is to anyone experiencing domestic abuse.

Breathe
Encourage
Achieve
Understand
Take care
Inspire
Forget
Unify
Leave

My Past

Over the years, I have made mistakes.
I have made wrong decisions, chosen the wrong things.
I have taken bad turns and walked the wrong paths.
Through all of those things, however bad they were —
they have taught me something.
I have learnt lessons.
Whichever way we get through each day, remember there will be happy times.
Tomorrow is another day, and each day we get through is another lesson learnt.

My Strength

I came to jail homeless and on a script of 90ml methadone but I am reducing, alongside my friend. We are helping each other and coming off it together. I am now on 35ml and hope to be off my script by my release.

Every time I have been released from prison, all I need is a stable place to live, then I can rebuild my life and get my children back into my care. However, every time I leave, I'm homeless, with no stability. It makes everything harder.

I've been homeless before and slept rough, including sleeping in a tent in the harsh winter. During this time, I experienced a blood clot in my womb. I was pregnant at the time, and lost my son, who was stillborn. Homelessness is a big issue and it's the thing we need most, especially women.

However, I am strong. I keep going. Strength means keeping going every day, even if you are dragging yourself through. Even when you don't feel you have a purpose, keep going. You do have a purpose, just like I do. I have my kids and I will keep going for them.

My True Identity

Can you see what I see?
A broken body image, that's deep within me.
Can you see me hiding, my true identity?
All I want is to be happy, and feel fully free.
Not a life of pain or inner misery.
So please don't pass judgement, and say you disagree.
Because I've got no time for people, and their negativity.
I want to be someone I'm proud of, someone I can be.
To look forward to a future, that's full of positivity.
Looking into a mirror, seeing the reflection of me.
Smiling at the courage I've shown, with my true identity.

Never Look Down on Anybody

I came from a loving, hard-working and a close-knit family. I had three grown-up children and two granddaughters when I found myself in prison. My whole world fell apart. My grandson was born a day after I came to prison. I never thought I would get through it. I thought I would die in custody. But I survived with the help of my family and the girls I met along the way.

I used to watch TV and comment on what people had done. Now, I will never look down on anyone. I have learnt the hard way that the people in custody are some of the best people, and shouldn't be looked down on.

We all have our own story and our own truth. Never look down on anybody as you never know when your whole world will come crashing down — in the blink of an eye. I know from experience and it has changed me forever.

One Foot at a Time

This ain't that deep or personal at all.
Fourteen years, this is where I live, sunset to dawn fall.
In this cell where I rise, I stand tall.
Thinking about my wrongs,
thinking about my rights.
Motivated movement call to mind power.
This is what I planned and this ain't personal,
this is what it is.
Real life takes a hold and heaven knows, I've tried.
All the pain and how I've cried.
But there's hope, power in the palm,
guess I'm writing this with my hand.
Dealing with the feeling, you don't have a chance.
Demands in the greed for freedom.
Voices of old, tried to change my ways,
most days — addiction, I just ride the waves.
Sometimes I slip and slide, but I will never fall.
Cos over and over again, I never have to try,
to fly or swim.
I still move forward — I crawl.
After all, I've got time.
Baby steps, that's all.
One foot at a time.

Our Goals (Voices of Prisoners)

To continue to stay clean.

Help those less fortunate.

Be the best mam I can be.

Stay drug free.

To become a mental health worker.

Look after my mam.

Continue on my recovery journey.

Keep developing my skills in prison.

Become a support worker in the future and work with the homeless.

To not come back to prison once I am out!

Our Love

The day you said you loved me babe,
it made me feel so happy.
It made me feel safe.
Whether you go, or I do first,
I need you to know,
that my time on earth,
was the best it could be.
Because I loved you,
and you loved me.

Our Time

We are sitting in our pads,
day by day.
Thinking of some words,
that we can say.
The thoughts are there,
but I just can't say.
The sun is shining,
So, I keep on smiling.

Our Voices (Quotes from Prisoners)

Be thankful for how far you have come.

You are stronger than you think.

Be kind to yourself and love yourself.

Every trauma you go through — remember, it makes you stronger every time.

Sometimes you've got to fall before you fly.

Don't judge me. If you walked in my shoes, you would know how far I have come.

Help others as God helps me.

Never give up — there's always another way.

You can lock the locks but can't stop the clocks.

If it's no good, do as you should.

When you hit a dead end, try, try again.

You may have lost a lot, but you will always have more to give.

Never let anyone dull your sparkle.

What is meant to be, will be.

When you cry a tear, you know you are here.

Love is from the heart — don't fall apart.

Be humble, be beautiful, be kind.

Say something nice, if you have no advice.

Don't grumble more than your stomach!

Life is short. Stand tall and make the most of it!

I'm like Lego, I always rebuild.

I is what I is and I am what I am!

Fly like a dove, show yourself some love.

You can make your dreams come true when you wake up and pursue them.

Live your life, day by day. Take each step in a positive way.

The struggles you are going through today, is the strength you need for tomorrow.

When you are going through hell, keep going because you know you are going to come out the other end.

You can't change the past, but you can change the future.

What's in your past, makes you who you are today.

You are worthy, don't let your mistakes define you.

No matter what happens, there is always a way out.

You only fail when you stop trying.

The best view comes after the hardest climb.

If it doesn't challenge you, it won't change you.

If you need drink or drugs to enjoy your life to the fullest — then you're doing it wrong.

Drink and drugs infect the mind faster than bacteria.

If you want to make it, believe in yourself — anything is possible.

You can be anybody you want to be.

You never know how strong you are until being strong is the only choice you have.

Pain

Sentenced to life,
I never even carried a knife.
Easily led,
Nowhere to sleep,
or even my own bed.
Smoking those drugs always stopped the pain,
or even the feeling of not being fed.
Told what to do,
it didn't make any difference to me.
I was always blue.

PMA

In life, we all have our bad days. However, it's the good days we need to keep in mind.

Positive
Mental
Attitude

Shining

Drinking alcohol, taking drugs,
living life to the extreme.
Ruthless, reckless behaviour,
afraid of no danger,
like a pink Power Ranger.
What even am I?
I don't even know myself anymore.

I had lost everything. Most importantly, I had lost my family and friends. I realised that I was either going to end up dead or in prison. Dark and desperate to gain my life back. Here I am, thankfully, in prison. I say thankfully, because I dread to think how my parents would have been if I was found dead. It's the ones who we leave behind that suffer.

I am now fighting back. I am owning my addictions and everything I have done wrong. I have started being honest with myself and my parents and friends. I have told them that I didn't realise I needed help. Now I'm here, I realise it. I now hear my parents when they say I was created to shine, not to be a fraction of the real me.

Strength

Strength to me,
is what I know.
It makes me feel uplifted,
it helps me grow.
The strength I have,
is who I am.
It pushes me to do,
what I can.

Strength is…

A woman,
a man,
a mother.
Strength is…
courage,
survival,
determination.
Strength is…
honesty,
never giving up,
strength in numbers.
Strength is…
holding it together,
powerful,
loud.
Strength is…
hope,
belief,
staying strong.
Strength is…
true.
Strength is…
you.

Strong

Some say I am so strong for handling everything life has thrown at me.
The truth is, I wasn't strong at all. Because my coping mechanism was turning to drugs.
Right now, being drug free, I feel the strongest I have ever been.
Over time, I know I will eventually reach my goal.
Not to turn to drugs to help me feel better.
Growing stronger each day, so I can overcome my addiction.

The Beat

Lost my home, nowhere to go.
Wandering down a dark street,
I found the working beat.
At night, while most sleep,
the sound of scurrying feet,
wondering who you next meet.
Twenty pounds please,
this is the story of how crack,
took me to my knees.
At least for a brief moment,
when I smoke this, I'll feel free.
I'd always be gone by the morning.
Never let these normal people see the things,
that happen to us in these streets.
My love-hate relationship,
to working the beat.

The Butterfly

The caterpillar was small, timid, and shy,
until it took to its cocoon, hiding for some time.
After so long, it emerged — bright, colourful,
taking to the sky, bold and beautiful.
The butterfly learnt and it showed us,
that as women, we can all be amazing.
We can make anything possible.

The Future

I was born in Hartlepool and I have two sisters and two brothers. Sadly, both of my sisters have passed away, and one of my brothers has also died. I still have my mam, but my dad died. I lived with my mam in a flat. She's sixty-five years old and getting weaker with age. I'm her carer in lots of ways and we have a really close relationship.

I'm trying to have a better life and not get into trouble. I want to make her proud and I want to look after her. Getting into trouble meant that I lost my ten-year-old daughter, who is now in foster care. It happened after I went down the wrong path in life and got involved with alcohol and drugs. Substances ruined my life and now I just want to focus on my future goals.

I want to be back in Hartlepool, with my own place, still looking after my mam. A house that is comfortable and safe. I want recover and stay off drugs, feel happy, and get a good job. I know I can do it, for myself and my mam.

The Light Ahead

No matter how dark,
your road is ahead of you,
always stay focused,
on the light ahead.
No shadow from your past,
can hold you back.
You have got to dig deep,
to fight through,
and become the fighter,
you are today.

The Power of Words

I am passionate about poetry and writing. All of my life, I've found joy in jotting down my thoughts and demons I am fighting. Real people all over the world can turn things around.

I am a believer, that with dedication, I can do the same and be proud. And one day, I will help others like me. Needless to say, a good scribble of my thoughts onto paper, is my therapy. Now, let me tell you — I will read others and if nothing else, end this crisis where we don't speak out.

To my Wife

I loved you once,
I love you still.
I always have,
and I always will.

Unconditional Love

The rush of love, the tears that flow,
the feeling of joy that fills your heart.
Those perfect moments when your child is born,
it's those beautiful memories that will last forever.
That's the day your life's complete,
the greatest gift you will ever know.
The gift of love as your child shall grow.
The nights you spend gazing at your child as they sleep.
The pure unconditional love you feel will always show.
I can't believe this beautiful little baby is mine.
You're so precious to me; you mean the world to me.

What is Love?

Love is love.
Love is hard.
That's why me and you don't fall apart.
Love is real.
Love is true.
When I see love, I see me and you.
Love is different.
Love is kind.
Me and my girl are one of a kind.
Love is strange.
Love is wonderful.
Our love blossoms, unconditional.
Love is love, in so many ways.
Love also grows day by day.
Don't lose sight of what love is.
When you find it, it is the ultimate bliss.

Without

Without communication,
there is no relationship.
Without respect,
there is no love.
Without trust,
there is no reason to continue.
We lose these through drink and drugs.

Women in my Life (Voices of Prisoners)

My mum and grandma have both inspired me in my life. My grandma has had to work hard a lot of her life and has always been able to childmind for my mother. My mum has also been a hard worker and had to put up with me over the years. I imagine this hasn't been easy but she still loves me. She comes to visit me and looks after me — even from afar.

My nannas inspire me. They inspire me because they are amazing wives, mothers, nannas, and friends. They ran the homes: cooking, cleaning, and raising children. I thank them, for being good role models and for loving and caring for me and all our family. When I was taken from my mam and dad, my nanna took me in and looked after me. And they cared for my daughters when I turned to drugs. Amazing women. I am so grateful.

My mam inspired me growing up. She did so much and worked hard to feed and look after me and my siblings. It was inspirational and she just got on with it. If she were still alive, I would want to tell her that every day, I miss her. She was amazing and I am so grateful for all the hard work she did to give us the best life. I love you, Mam.

The woman who inspires me most is my mother-in-law. She is a very strong woman and has been through the mill in her own life; with abusive partners and a bad pregnancy, where she nearly lost her baby, as she was so poorly. She then had to have a liver transplant, yet, she is still going strong. She is my best friend as well as my mother-in-law. She always looks after me, even now I am in jail. I would like to thank her, from the bottom of my heart, and tell her that she is the best mother-in-law ever. Thank you, and I can't wait to see you for cake and coffee.

My nana inspired me and she was my best friend. She loved me and was the only one who kept me safe in life. She went through hell and back in her younger years and fought through. My nana was the strongest woman I knew and from having nothing in life, she ended up having everything. She used to take me on holiday and I have lovely memories. I wish she had never died in my darkest time in life, because I never would have struggled so badly. My nana was beautiful, kind, caring, and she taught me all the tools in life to be a good person and have a good heart.

Women

Women are wonderful,
Obviously.
Men are not as strong as us.
Every woman,
Needs to be loved and treat right.

Women's Day

Women are worth it.
One and only, we can
Make life on earth.
Every woman is unique.
Not all of a woman's
Skills are appreciated.

Decide for yourself.
Always believe in yourself.
You're worth it.

Words

Once the words leave your mouth,
you can never take them back.
Be careful what you say,
words hurt.
But when you are in despair,
your family will always be there.

Your Own Strength

Regret is a word we all know well.
Before regret consumes us, try changing tomorrow…
TODAY!
You might feel defenceless,
but you don't know what your own strength is.

Acknowledgements

Thank you to the prisoners at HMP Low Newton. It was a privilege to be trusted with your words and experiences. I am thankful that you welcomed me into the prison and participated in the sessions. Your stories and reflections have left an impact on me, and I know they will touch other people. Thank you for sharing.

A big thank you to all the staff at Novus and HMPPS for welcoming me in at Low Newton and providing support and encouragement. You all do an amazing job and you all make a difference.

Thank you to the National Lottery Community Fund for providing a grant that enabled Write on the Tyne to run the project of well-being writing in HMP Low Newton.

Special thanks to Alison and Johnny Harrison, who allowed the production and distribution of this book through nominating Write on the Tyne to receive funding at their wedding. Thank you to those who donated: Brenda Giles, Linda Giles, Cheryl Giles, Maura Dent, Mike and Stina Porter, Chris, Sheila, and Michael Dangerfield, Venetia and Peter McMahon, Karen White, Kristofer, Laura Linden, Kelly Lumley, Jaelin Farrow, Brendan and Rachel O'Reilly, Natasha Mcintyre, Caroline Myers, Jasmine Addlesee, and Ian Cramond. Your gift will make a huge difference.

For more information about Write on the Tyne (CIC) visit: www.writeonthetyne.com